MY BALLET BOOK

Written by KATE CASTLE

DK PUBLISHING, INC.

A DK PUBLISHING BOOK

Editor Melanie Halton **Designer** Emma Bowden

Senior Editor Fiona Robertson **Senior Art Editor** Rebecca Johns

Managing Editor Mary Ling

Managing Art Editor Rachael Foster

US Editor Constance M. Robinson **Photographer** Patrick Baldwin

DTP Designer Andrew O'Brien

Production Kate Oliver

Picture Research Angela Anderson

First American Edition, 1998

2 4 6 8 10 9 7 5 3 1

Published in the United States by
DK Publishing, Inc.
95 Madison Avenue, New York, New York 10016

Visit us on the World Wide Web at http://www.dk.com

Copyright © 1998 Dorling Kindersley Limited, London

Library of Congress Cataloging-in-Publication Data

Castle, Kate.
   My ballet book: an introduction to the magical world of ballet /
by Kate Castle. – 1st American ed.
      p.   cm.
   Includes index.
   Summary: Introduces the world of ballet and presents its notable
stories, dancers, techniques, and routines.
   ISBN 0-7894-3432-6
   1. Ballet – Juvenile literature. 2. Ballet dancing – Juvenile
literature.   [1. Ballet dancing. 2. Ballet.]   I. Title.
GV1787.5.C372   1998
792.8–dc21
                                            98-22803 CIP AC

Color reproduction by Colourscan, Singapore   Printed and bound in Italy by L.E.G.O.

Contents

DISCOVERING BALLET

BALLET IS A WAY of dancing known for its beauty, lightness, and grace. It delights audiences by combining dance, music, scenery, and costuming to tell stories or create a particular mood. Although ballet has been handed down over generations of dancers and teachers, it is constantly evolving. As choreographers create new ballets, they use existing steps, called ballet technique, in many different ways. New ballets therefore use both traditional steps and exciting new movements to reflect today's world.

No strain must show in the arms or shoulders.

The dancer's legs are strong but extended into a graceful line with a pointed toe.

Strength

Ballet is delightful to watch because of its lightness and strength. An exuberant jump like this seems to defy gravity. But it takes hard work and great technical skill. An important part of the dancer's training is to learn to make dancing seem effortless in performance.

This leg must stay turned out in the air.

Ready to dance

Everyone can enjoy learning ballet. But to be a professional dancer you need to be well proportioned, with good muscle tone and bone structure. Combined with proper training, this will help to avoid injury later. This dancer is fit, streamlined, and looks ready to dance.

Thigh muscles must not be overdeveloped.

Lift up out of the waist and twist.

Feet are turned out in first position.

Exercise

Dancers learn body conditioning and fitness exercises to make them more supple and to build stamina. They work to strengthen the parts of their body that are weaker than others. Before daily class, they will do some of these exercises on their own, to warm up their muscles.

Studio work

Daily practice is essential for both beginners and famous dancers alike. The studio should have a *barre*, mirrors around the walls for you to check your placing (see page 14), and a wood or vinyl floor. Classes aim to build strength, suppleness, and stamina. Dancers know that if they miss class one day, they will notice it, two days and their teacher will notice, three days and their audience will surely notice!

Contents

DISCOVERING BALLET

BALLET IS A WAY of dancing known for its beauty, lightness, and grace. It delights audiences by combining dance, music, scenery, and costuming to tell stories or create a particular mood. Although ballet has been handed down over generations of dancers and teachers, it is constantly evolving. As choreographers create new ballets, they use existing steps, called ballet technique, in many different ways. New ballets therefore use both traditional steps and exciting new movements to reflect today's world.

No strain must show in the arms or shoulders.

The dancer's legs are strong but extended into a graceful line with a pointed toe.

Strength
Ballet is delightful to watch because of its lightness and strength. An exuberant jump like this seems to defy gravity. But it takes hard work and great technical skill. An important part of the dancer's training is to learn to make dancing seem effortless in performance.

This leg must stay turned out in the air.

Ready to dance
Everyone can enjoy learning ballet. But to be a professional dancer you need to be well proportioned, with good muscle tone and bone structure. Combined with proper training, this will help to avoid injury later. This dancer is fit, streamlined, and looks ready to dance.

Thigh muscles must not be overdeveloped.

Lift up out of the waist and twist.

Exercise
Dancers learn body conditioning and fitness exercises to make them more supple and to build stamina. They work to strengthen the parts of their body that are weaker than others. Before daily class, they will do some of these exercises on their own, to warm up their muscles.

Feet are turned out in first position.

Studio work
Daily practice is essential for both beginners and famous dancers alike. The studio should have a *barre*, mirrors around the walls for you to check your placing (see page 14), and a wood or vinyl floor. Classes aim to build strength, suppleness, and stamina. Dancers know that if they miss class one day, they will notice it, two days and their teacher will notice, three days and their audience will surely notice!

Profile of a dancer

Every young dancer dreams of joining a professional ballet company and performing on stage wearing wonderful costumes. To become successful, dancers must be intelligent and adaptable. They have to be able to cope with the physical and technical demands of ballet. They should also be sensitive to music and able to express different emotions. Most of all, they must love to dance in front of an audience!

Tiny net sleeves make it easy for the dancer to move her arms.

Both arms are outstretched to the audience.

An upturned palm says "thank you."

Feet are placed together.

Révérence

At the end of class and performances, dancers make a *révérence*, or bow, as a way of saying thank you to their teacher and pianist. On stage, dancers learn to share their enjoyment of ballet with the audience, and the audience in turn shows its appreciation with applause. Ballet would not exist without audiences.

A long graceful neck makes port de bras (see page 12) more beautiful.

This dancer is wearing a practice skirt over her leotard.

This tutu comes from the Romantic ballet Les Sylphides (see page 30).

Dancing with a partner

An important and enjoyable part of ballet is dancing with a partner, or *pas de deux*. It begins when the dancer's own technique (the ability to perform steps) is secure and accomplished. Dancers have to be aware of the shape they are making in relation to their partner.

This dancer's supporting foot is beautifully turned out on pointe.

DRESSED TO DANCE

WHILE YOU ARE LEARNING to dance, you will wear close-fitting practice clothes. This is so that your teacher can see your movements clearly. Loose clothing makes it harder to see whether you are properly placed and are developing a sense of "line" (see page 17). Most ballet schools like their pupils to wear uniform practice clothes. For examinations, you need to be particularly neat and well presented.

Neat box
It's a good idea to keep everything neat in a small carrying case that you can take to class, examinations, and performances. Fill it with pins, barrettes, a comb, hair net, hair spray, elastics, spare shoe ribbons, small scissors, needles, and thread.

Scooped necklines create graceful neck and shoulder lines.

Always remove any jewelry before you dance, because it could catch on clothing.

Practice wear
Younger girls wear a leotard, perhaps with a short wraparound skirt, and pink or white anklets. Younger boys wear black shorts and a white T-shirt and white socks. Older girls wear pink tights and older boys wear dark tights with a white T-shirt on top, or a leotard underneath. Older male students can wear all-over body tights.

Belts help teachers to check placing and alignment.

Make sure your nails are clean and short and never wear nail polish, particularly on stage.

Hair spray and hair nets keep stray wisps in place.

Boys wear white socks over dark tights.

Neat hair
If you have short hair, you can pin it back or wear a headband. Long hair has to be pinned up securely in a bun or French twist.

Jazz shoes

Men's character shoes

Women's character shoes

Men's leather shoes with elastic

Pointe shoes with ribbons

Leather shoes with ribbons

Satin shoes with ribbons

Men's soft boots

Tying ribbons

1 Use either nylon or satin ribbons. Keep your foot flat on the floor and take the inside ribbon around to the back of the ankle.

2 Wrap the ribbon around the front of the ankle and then to the back again. Flex your ankle to make sure the ribbon is not too tight.

3 Take hold of the other ribbon and pass this over the first one and around the ankle. Try not to let the first ribbon slip.

4 Bring the ends of the two ribbons to the inside of your ankle and tie them in a neat knot.

5 The ends should be about 2 in (4 cm) long. Trim new ribbons to size after you have tied them and then tuck the ends in neatly.

Performance dress
Many ballet performances feature tutus, and students learning *pas de deux* often wear a tutu so that they and their partners can get used to working with it.

Tutu skirt is worn over a practice leotard.

Dancing shoes
There are different types of shoes for different styles of dancing. For example, male dancers can wear soft leather boots over tights.

Take care not to sew through the drawstring.

Fold the heel over and stitch the elastic at the crease.

Sewing elastics
In class you will be allowed to wear soft shoes with an elastic, but you need ribbons for exams and performances. Stitch about 1 in (2 cm) of the elastic to each side of the shoe. Make sure the elastic is not too tight.

If you darn the toes of the shoes, they will last longer.

Pointe shoes
Your teacher will tell you when you are ready to wear *pointe* shoes. They must be fitted properly in a special store. Sew satin ribbons in the same place as you sew your elastics. When you get new shoes, you can remove the old ribbons, wash them, and use them again.

Tuck in the drawstring neatly.

11

BASIC POSITIONS

THERE ARE FIVE BASIC POSITIONS of the feet and arms in ballet. Every step begins and ends with one of these positions. When a series of steps are linked together, they make *enchaînements*. Many *enchaînements* put together by a choreographer to tell a story or create a mood makes a ballet. Every choreographer will use these basic positions, so your teacher will spend a lot of time making sure that you have learned them correctly.

Hand positions

Hands are an important part of the beautiful "line" created by the body and should always be graceful and expressive. Group your fingers together softly, or stretch them into *allongé* in the *arabesque* position. Be aware of your hands as you dance and try not to let them show the strain when you are working hard.

Five basic feet positions

1 In **first position**, your heels are touching and your toes are turned out to the side. You may find it difficult to turn your feet out this far at first, so begin with each foot turned out 45°. Make sure that your legs are turned out from the hips.

2 In **second position**, stand with your feet a shoulder-width apart. Make sure your weight is evenly placed in the middle and stand up straight.

3 Place the heel of one foot in front of the middle of your other foot for **third position**. This position is used only when you are first learning ballet, as a stage toward learning fifth position, which is much harder.

4 This is a crossed **fourth position**, which is used as a preparation for *pirouettes*. Place one foot in front of the other, with a space the length of your foot between them.

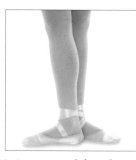

5 Put the heel of your front foot against the toe of the back foot for **fifth position**. This is the hardest position of all because it demands good turnout with straight legs and correct posture.

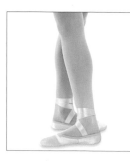

Basic arm positions

You will learn the basic arm positions as fixed positions to begin with, then as a series of flowing movements. Gradually you will put them with movements that use the whole body to bend, turn, jump, and travel.

Don't let your wrists droop.

1 Hold your hands apart slightly, with your fingers softly grouped. Keep your hands away from your body, as if you are wearing a costume that shouldn't be crushed.

2 Your arms and hands should slope naturally downward from your shoulders in a smooth curve. Hold them a little to the front of your body and don't let your elbows droop.

Port de bras

The term *port de bras* means "carriage of the arms" and it describes the continuous flow of arm movements through the basic positions. *Port de bras* gives dancing grace and expression. There are several organizations that promote the study of ballet. Each will have its own syllabus or set of steps, which differs slightly from the others. The Cecchetti method is named after the great teacher, Enrico Cecchetti, who taught many famous dancers. The *port de bras* shown here is similar to one Cecchetti would have taught.

Shoulders should be placed square in relation to the hips.

1 Move slowly and smoothly through all these positions. Count one-two-three-four until you reach the last.

Basic hand position

Allongé

5 Bring both arms up to form a frame around your face. Try to relax your shoulders or the strain will show in your hands.

Hold your shoulder back, in line with the hip. If you let it come forward, your body will twist.

Palms face inward so that your little finger forms the outside curve of the shape.

Hold your wrist in a soft curve so as not to break the "line."

Keep your hips level, not twisted or lifted, and your weight evenly placed.

3 Hold one arm curved in front of your body and the other out to the side, as in second position. Make sure the arm does not cross over too far. This position is often used to prepare for a *pirouette*.

4 Keeping one arm in front of you, raise the other arm. You can perform all five positions in any direction, which adds interest. The way your body relates to space is called alignment.

2 Place your arms in second position and your feet in fourth on a *plié*. This is a transitional position.

Use your back arm to balance.

3 Transfer your weight onto the back foot, and sweep one arm across the front of your body.

4 Place your weight evenly between your feet and bring your arms forward.

5 Face the corner with the left leg in front. This position is called "croisé," or crossed.

Lift up out of the waist and look out toward the audience from the frame around your head.

Don't let the insteps or knees roll forward as you make a plié.

BEGINNING BALLET

TAKING BALLET LESSONS can be exciting and challenging. It is always important to find a good teacher who is fully qualified. This is because your body is still growing and needs careful training. Some schools offer examinations to monitor progress, and give performances for parents and friends to enjoy. At first you will probably only need one lesson each week, but as you improve you may want to take more, or try other styles of dance. Between classes, you could practice simple exercises at home.

Starting position for pliés

Keep your shoulders relaxed throughout these exercises.

Holding the barre
The *barre* is a smooth wooden rail that gives support while you practice your steps. Hold it lightly at about waist height. Try not to grab at it or grip too hard, or the strain will show in your dancing.

Remember to relax your facial muscles.

Keeping your elbow low, place your hand slightly in front of you.

Barre warm-ups
The first exercise you will do at the *barre* is a *plié*. "Plier" means to bend or fold. It is useful for warming up, gives strength and flexibility, and is a good preparation for other steps, including jumps. You can practice *pliés* holding onto the *barre* with both hands, so that your shoulders and hips are level.

Perfect posture
You can draw an imaginary vertical line from this dancer's heels up to the top of her head. Try to stand as naturally as possible. Pull the tummy in and the bottom up. Keep the head straight and the eyes and chin level.

Keep the back straight and shoulders relaxed.

Shoulders relaxed

Working with a teacher
In class, the teacher is there to help – to give praise when you are working hard, and to correct your mistakes. At the *barre*, the teacher checks placing, which is the relationship of one part of the body to another. This teacher is showing the dancer how to turn out her leg in *petit battement.*

Pull up the kneecaps.

Knee must point to the side.

Feet are turned out in first position.

Weight is placed over the front part of the foot.

Petit battement

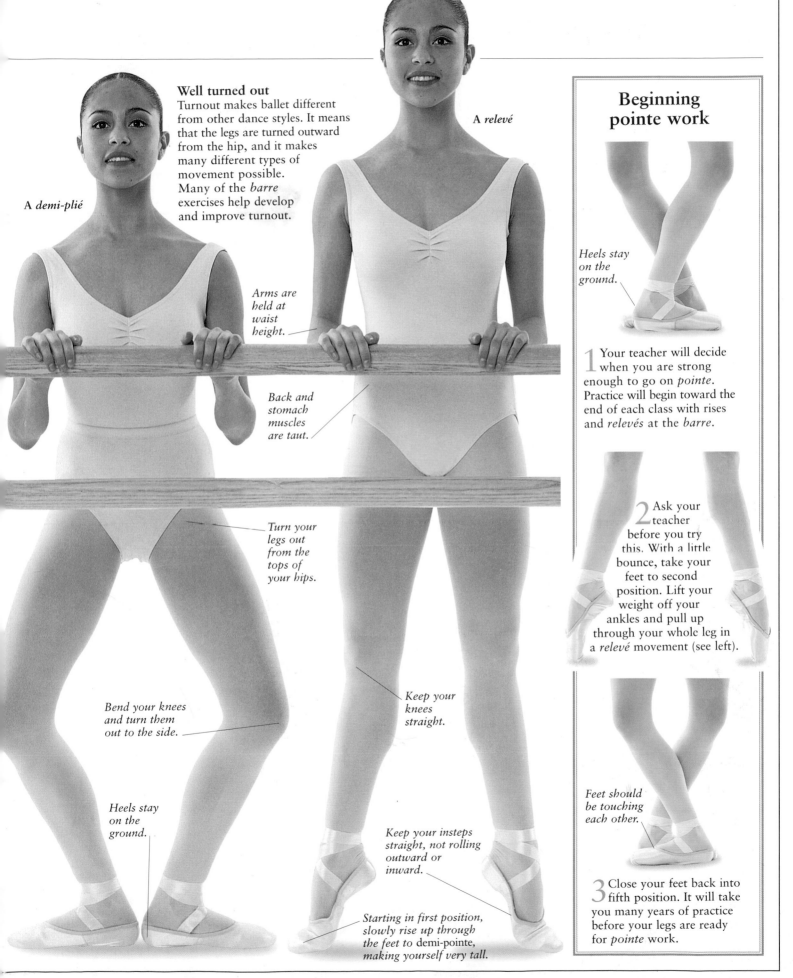

A *demi-plié*

Well turned out
Turnout makes ballet different from other dance styles. It means that the legs are turned outward from the hip, and it makes many different types of movement possible. Many of the *barre* exercises help develop and improve turnout.

A *relevé*

Arms are held at waist height.

Back and stomach muscles are taut.

Turn your legs out from the tops of your hips.

Bend your knees and turn them out to the side.

Keep your knees straight.

Heels stay on the ground.

Keep your insteps straight, not rolling outward or inward.

Starting in first position, slowly rise up through the feet to demi-pointe, making yourself very tall.

Beginning pointe work

Heels stay on the ground.

1 Your teacher will decide when you are strong enough to go on *pointe*. Practice will begin toward the end of each class with rises and *relevés* at the *barre*.

2 Ask your teacher before you try this. With a little bounce, take your feet to second position. Lift your weight off your ankles and pull up through your whole leg in a *relevé* movement (see left).

Feet should be touching each other.

3 Close your feet back into fifth position. It will take you many years of practice before your legs are ready for *pointe* work.

AT THE BARRE

THE PURPOSE OF *BARRE* EXERCISES is to prepare for work in the center of the studio, and eventually on stage. Each exercise follows a pattern that will help to build strength, skill, and stamina. It is quite usual to spend 30 minutes at the *barre*, followed by an hour of practice in the center. Although it can seem repetitive, *barre* work should be performed with musicality and a sense of enjoyment, as if dancing on stage. All professional dancers, no matter how famous, take class every working day and may perform the same *barre* exercises again as an essential warm-up before performances.

Hold your arm in a soft curve.

Développé

A *développé* is a smooth unfolding of the leg through a series of positions. This exercise is more advanced and is a preparation for slow, sustained movements, called *adagio*. The ability to raise and hold an extended leg in the air is called "extension."

Arm is in first position.

Hold the barre lightly as you lift your leg.

Leg is turned out from the hip right through to the toe.

1 Lift the foot from fifth position to touch the ankle. This position is called *sur le cou de pied* (on the neck of the foot or ankle).

2 Raise the foot to the knee in a *retiré*. Keep the hip level – do not lift it with the leg.

3 This is a *développé à la seconde*. At first, the height of a *développé* is less important than turnout and being properly placed. You should start your turnout at 45° and aim for 90°.

Battement tendu

This is quite a simple exercise and usually comes after *pliés*. It uses all the leg muscles and strengthens the feet and legs for footwork and traveling steps.

There is an open feeling across the chest.

Make your neck long and elegant.

Try not to let your body drop on this side at the barre.

1 Begin in fifth position with your arm raised to second. The exercise is performed *en croix*, which means it is performed to the front, to the side, to the back, and to the side again, in the shape of a cross.

2 Stretch your foot to point to the front, *devant*. Your heel should lead. Do not place any weight on your front foot. Try to turn your leg out from the hip.

3 Close back smoothly into fifth position. Try not to wriggle. Keep your legs straight and your tummy lifted, and concentrate on the next part of the exercise.

Keep the feet fully crossed and touching.

Attitude effacée derrière

An *attitude* is a position where one leg is lifted and bent, either to the front – *devant* – or behind – *derrière*. The position shown here is an open (*effacée*) position, where the leg nearest the audience is raised.

Follow the line made by your arm with your head.

Hold the arm in fifth position in a soft curve to accentuate the position.

There is an invisible straight line from your back down to your supporting heel and up to the top of your head.

Your foot should be level with your knee in this kind of attitude.

Back foot is stretched to a beautiful point, emphasizing the "line."

The whole supporting leg is well turned out.

Battement fondu derrière

Fondu means "melted" and this exercise combines *pliés* with a gentle stretching of the leg to build up strength and control. As performed here, it looks like an *arabesque* with the leg lifted 45° and the body facing in toward the *barre*. It is performed *en croix*, and can also be performed *en relevé*.

Turn your head to face the side.

4 Slide your foot out strongly to the side, then close to fifth behind. Make the *battement tendu* to the back and then repeat to the side. Turn around and repeat the exercise with the other leg.

This foot is the supporting foot and should be turned out.

Arabesque penchée

One of the best-known and most beautiful positions in ballet is the *arabesque*. In an *arabesque*, your body makes a long line from the top of your finger to the tip of your toe. An *arabesque* is a good illustration of one of the most important features of classical ballet – the invisible lines and curves that can be traced through the shapes the dancer's body makes in space. The *penchée*, or inclined *arabesque*, will take a great deal of practice.

Working leg is absolutely straight.

Lift your kneecap but do not let your weight fall too far back.

Take care not to let the body drop too far forward.

Arm is held delicately in the arabesque position to continue the "line." It should show no strain.

The instep on your supporting foot is raised en relevé.

Your supporting foot must not roll inward.

17

LIFE AT A BALLET SCHOOL

IF YOU WANT to become a professional dancer, you need to go to a senior school, such as English National Ballet School, which offers intensive training for students from 16 to 19 years old. Students come from all over the world and are selected at auditions. They must have a good physique, excellent ballet technique, and the potential to become professional performers. The School also offers training in other types of dance, such as jazz, tap, character, and *pas de deux*. Many students go on to join English National Ballet or other ballet companies.

A well-rounded education
Students study a range of academic and dance-related subjects at English National Ballet School. These include history, notation, and anatomy. Students also study music and art, because it is important for dancers to have an all-around understanding of the arts. They are encouraged to see a wide range of dance performances.

Preparing for classes
The School places great importance on students looking well groomed and professional. The dressing room is warm and spacious. There are lockers for each student, and showers for use after class. Mirrors have lights around them, just as in theater dressing rooms.

The students study other dance performances on video.

The ballet teacher works with the fitness consultant to prepare each student's program.

Keeping fit
Fitness and stamina are essential for dancers. The school has a body conditioning studio, which the students can use between classes. Programs designed to strengthen their bodies are specially prepared by a fitness consultant. This training is particularly useful while recovering from injury.

The physiotherapist uses a range of treatments to heal muscle injuries.

Tutu stand

Costumes for practice and performances should always be stored neatly when they are not being used. The School has devised this ingenious stand as a way of keeping tutus in perfect condition.

The tutus are put onto the stand upside down to stop the layers from getting crushed.

Caring for injuries

When students are injured, they can have physiotherapy sessions. The physiotherapist may be a former dancer, who will understand the dancer's concerns.

Between classes

The day usually begins at nine and ends after five. Breaks are therefore important, not just to rest, but also to get to know the other students. The School encourages students to eat properly, get enough sleep, and generally take responsibility for their own good health.

Fruit and vegetables provide vitamins and minerals, which are an essential part of a dancer's healthy diet.

Studio work

The most important part of the day is class. This is taught by experienced former principal dancers who have trained to teach at this level. The teacher will demonstrate as he or she sets an exercise, then watch as the students dance in small groups. Students use the mirror to make sure their positions are correct, but must not become too dependent on it.

School's out

Students always look at the bulletin board on arrival. The bulletin board is the focal point of the School. It shows the weekly timetable, which guest teachers are visiting the school, and other news items. Dance training is very tiring, but like other young people, dancers enjoy going out with their friends at the end of the day.

STUDIO TO STAGE

CENTER PRACTICE FOLLOWS *barre* work and prepares a dancer for performing on stage. All the steps vary in speed, direction, and type of movement, which makes them interesting to watch and perform. Center practice follows a set pattern. It begins with *port de bras* exercises, then *adagio*, *pirouettes* (turns), *petits allegro* (little jumps), *batterie* (beating steps) and finally, *grands allegro* (large jumps).

Eyes look along the arm and toward the hand.

Fully extended foot creates a smooth "line."

Petits allegro
Small, neat steps such as *jetés*, *entrechats*, and *brisé volés* give the impression of lightness and speed when put together in sequence. A particularly light and bouncy way of jumping is called *"ballon."*

Batterie
A *brisé volé* is a virtuoso, or especially skillful, beating step.

Body bends toward the legs.

Feet pass quickly in front and behind each other in a stretched jump.

The dancer looks into the distance, as if trying to capture something just out of reach.

Pas de deux
This graceful shape combines some of the basic positions of the arms and feet. This position is called a fish dive.

Adagio
The *arabesques* practiced at the *barre* and in the center now move on stage. This *arabesque* is from the ballet *Les Sylphides*, created by Michel Fokine, and is called "first *arabesque*." It has a feeling of great delicacy and charm and the "line" is very clear.

Pirouette
Turns are either in place or traveling in a series. To avoid dizziness, dancers use a focusing technique called "spotting."

Stay focused on the object.

Refocus on the object.

Find something to focus on.

1 Begin in fourth position, with your weight evenly placed, left foot in front, and arms in third. Pick up the back foot and turn sharply to the right.

2 Make a *relevé* with the right foot lifted in a well turned-out *retiré* to the left knee. Keep looking toward the front.

3 Quickly bring your head around to look ahead again. Finish the turn in a neat fifth position, facing the front.

Some weight is on the back foot to help balance.

Supported adagio

Pas de deux needs strength and precision and both dancers play equally important roles. This supported *arabesque* has a very different feeling from the solo *arabesque* – less wistful and more regal.

Back arm is stretched to create a continuous "line" with the front arm.

Grands allegro

An exciting part of *grands allegro* is a dramatic *grand jeté*. The dancers' arms are lifted to help them jump and make it look like they are flying.

Front arm is stretched, fingers allongé.

The dancer's arms are lifted and his body is curved, to look like a salmon jumping out of water.

Grands allegro

In *The Sleeping Beauty*, the Bluebird dances a virtuoso solo, which includes both *brisé volés* and *temps de poisson*. *Temps de poisson* is meant to look like a fish jumping out of water. The dancer jumps high in the air with both legs held together.

This is also a first arabesque. Being on pointe makes the position more streamlined and extended.

It is very important to avoid letting the effort show in the face or arms.

Arm is curved softly in fifth position.

The foot is pointed and taken as high as possible.

Hold your arm in a relaxed second position.

Pointe work

After simple exercises at the *barre*, *pointe* work is perfected in the center. The dancer lifts her weight up out of her hips and off her feet, to avoid hurting her toes.

The supporting leg is well turned out.

Foot is raised to the knee in retiré.

Développé en pointe

This *développé à la seconde* demands extension, poise, strength, and expressiveness, all combined in one swiftly unfolding movement. It is an example of female virtuosity.

PLAYING THE PART

BﾠALLET USES a mixture of ballet technique, mime, and natural body language to tell stories. Newer ballets mainly use ballet steps and more natural movement to convey meaning, while the earlier ballets, such as *Swan Lake* and *Giselle*, use traditional mime. Mime is a conversation that uses gestures instead of words. The gestures are as precise as ballet steps and have to be learned and performed accurately.

Using mime

The story shown here was created using ballet mime gestures. The dancers are using their whole bodies to tell the story and each mime gesture flows smoothly from one to another. Think of how you use your own body and facial expressions to let people know if you are frightened, angry, or puzzled. Ballet has exaggerated these gestures so that they can be seen on stage.

Body language

Watching ballet is more interesting when you look at the movements and positions and use your imagination to understand what is happening. This picture shows how costume and dance combine with body language to create a character. The pose is from *Swan Lake*. The dancer holds her arms behind her like swan's wings. The tutu she is wearing adds to the image of the swan on the lake. She is looking down, which suggests that she is either frightened or shy.

Arms are gently arched and lifted.

Softly extended fingers

On stage, the swan wears a white feathered headdress with diamonds, to suggest drops of water.

Pointed and stretched foot forms a smooth, streamlined shape.

She gently shakes her raised fists.

1 A prince and princess meet in the forest. The princess tells the prince that she has met an angry man.

"WHY ARE YOU HERE?"

"THERE IS AN ANGRY MAN."

Open arms convey a question.

"I AM AFRAID."

"DON'T BE AFRAID."

She steps aside and moves her hands, as if pushing him away.

He crosses his wrists while shaking his head.

2 The princess tells the prince she is afraid. He tells her she has nothing to fear.

Eyes are raised.

"I WILL SAVE YOU."

Palms are turned upward.

She turns to face the prince.

3 Lifting his arms gently above his head, as if raising something from the ground, the prince conveys that he will save the princess. Feeling less afraid, the princess turns toward the prince.

An open-palm gesture shows honesty and trust.

"I PROMISE AND SWEAR TO KEEP MY PROMISE."

"I WILL MARRY YOU."

Hand on heart means making a promise.

She points to her finger to show that she will marry the prince.

4 The princess asks the prince if they will marry. The prince promises that he will wed the princess and swears to keep his promise.

The art of mime

Mime has been handed down from one famous dancer to another, so learning mime is like becoming a part of history. The mime gestures shown here are still used in ballet today.

Reading

In Coppélia, Swanilda tells us she sees the doll, Coppélia, reading a book.

Sleeping

In The Sleeping Beauty, *the Lilac Fairy shows that Aurora will sleep.*

Death

In Giselle, *the wicked Queen of the Wilis tells Prince Albrecht he must dance until he dies.*

Begging or pleading

Giselle pleads with the Queen of the Wilis to save Prince Albrecht, whom she loves and hopes to marry.

In La Sylphide, *the Sylphide listens for the footsteps of James, the young man who loves her.*

Hearing

JOINING A COMPANY

EVERY DANCER DREAMS of joining a ballet company. If there is an advanced school attached to the company, some of the students may graduate into the company, but dancers are usually chosen at auditions. Everyone begins in the *corps de ballet*, but can become soloists or principals if they work hard in class and perform well on stage. Their day is long, beginning with class in the morning, and ending with the performance – sometimes two if there is an afternoon matinée. There are also rehearsals and costume fittings with rest breaks in between. The company is like a family that spends a lot of time together, rehearsing, traveling, and performing.

Running a company

Many people are involved in the running of a busy ballet company. At the head is a Director, who decides which ballets are to be performed. Administrators deal with booking tours, travel arrangements, and salaries. The music staff includes conductors, orchestral players, and accompanists for rehearsals. The ballet staff organizes rehearsal schedules and prepares cast sheets, listing who will dance which parts.

Widow Simone dancing the clog dance in La Fille mal gardée

Sugar Plum Fairy

Senior artists

Although a dancer's performing career can be quite short, some older dancers continue to perform on stage in dramatic parts. Many dancers join the staff of the company as teachers. They may teach daily class or become répétiteurs, coaching and teaching new roles.

Rehearsals

When the company is on tour, daily class may take place on stage, followed by rehearsals. There are several casts for each ballet, and each will need a rehearsal. The final run-through with costumes, scenery, and orchestra is called a "dress rehearsal." On tour, each stage is different, so rehearsals called "placing calls" walk dancers through the steps to allow them to get used to the new stage.

The corps de ballet *from* The Sleeping Beauty *dances together.*

Corps de ballet

The dancers who perform together as a group are known as the *corps de ballet*. The *corps de ballet* must move like one dancer, not many individuals. This can take hours of rehearsal with the ballet master or mistress. Some dancers choose to remain in the *corps de ballet* because they enjoy the precision of the movements involved, and like working as part of a team. The *corps de ballet* features prominently in more traditional ballets, such as *The Sleeping Beauty* and *Swan Lake*.

Dr. Coppélius, the doll maker from the ballet Coppélia

Character soloists
These roles require dramatic as well as dancing ability. The character of Dr. Coppélius, the doll maker from *Coppélia*, is created using costume, makeup, mime, and acting.

The headdress is decorated with feathers to give it a birdlike appearance.

Male soloist
The Bluebird character from *The Sleeping Beauty* is a male solo role. Soloists are coached by répétiteurs who have danced the role themselves.

The brisé volé *shown here makes the soloist look as though he is flying.*

Nutcracker Prince

This pas de deux *is from* The Nutcracker.

Female soloist
A female soloist, or *coryphée*, dances important roles, and may be an understudy for principal roles. Not all companies use the category *coryphée*. Some prefer the term junior soloist. Dancers in this category perform solos, but also dance in the *corps de ballet*.

Principals
The highest-ranking dancers are called principals and senior principals. They dance the leading roles in ballets and may perform only once or twice a week. A female principal can also be called a ballerina. Principals often create roles in new ballets, with soloists acting as understudies. Sometimes, principals are invited to visit other companies as guest artists.

Working together
Once the curtain has gone up, everyone works together: principals, soloists, senior artists, and *corps de ballet*. They dance to create a moving scene that will captivate their audience.

BACKSTAGE

I N THE SAME WAY that a dancer has to make ballet technique appear effortless to the audience, it is up to the backstage staff to create a magical world on stage. During a performance there is constant activity behind the scenes. Dressers help dancers make quick costume changes, scenery is moved by the stage crew, and lighting and sound are checked by technicians. Everyone works together to make the performance perfect. The people behind the scenes seldom take a bow, yet they are still working hard after the performance, making sure that everything is ready for the next show.

Costumes waiting for repair are hung on racks in the wardrobe.

Wardrobe staff works constantly behind the scenes, altering and repairing costumes.

Warming up
Dancers always warm up before the show to prevent injury. Before the curtain rises, the stage is full of dancers stretching and practicing difficult steps. They will all be nervous, because they want to dance their very best for the audience.

A perfect fit
A costume really helps a dancer to become the character that he or she is dancing. The dancer tries on every new costume for the designer and the dressmaker to make sure it is easy to move in and gives the effect the designer intended. Costumes are only worn for stage rehearsals, not in the studio.

Ballet wardrobe
The production wardrobe works from designs to make up the elaborate costumes, and the running wardrobe does repairs and maintenance. Costumes may even need emergency repairs during the performance. The wardrobe staff has usually studied how to design and make costumes at colleges that run courses on theater design.

This wig is worn by the Ice Queen in The Nutcracker.

Wig block

A head of hair
Between performances wigs are placed on a wig block and are restyled using heated rollers and curling irons. Wig-makers are trained hairdressers who have specialized in wig-making.

Making a point
Every female dancer uses at least ten pairs of *pointe* shoes a month. Ballet shoes are often dyed to match the costumes. This is done by the shoe supervisor, who orders all the shoes – boots, *pointes*, and character – from the makers and looks after them. A company may use 1.5 miles (2.5 km) of ribbon each year for its ballet shoes.

The Nutcracker Doll

Running the show
The stage manager runs the show from the "prompt corner." He or she calls dancers to the stage from the dressing rooms and coordinates the work of the front-of-house staff and the stage technicians.

This dancer has still to put on her wig and headdress.

These stage technicians are using a rope and pulley to change a backdrop.

Close at hand
Properties, called props, are the objects that dancers carry in their hands during a performance. Props are kept in a room close to the stage, and are cared for by the property master. During a performance, they are put on a table in the wings – the area at the side of the stage.

Setting the scene
Scenery is moved either by hand or by electrical machinery. Backdrops can be raised by rope and pulley, while others are lowered into place. Moving large pieces of scenery in this way is called "flying."

The lighting manager makes sure the preprogrammed light changes operate smoothly.

The ballet mistress shows the dancer where to place her foot sur le cou de pied *(on the neck of the foot or ankle).*

Understudies
Occasionally, a dancer may be injured just before a performance, so another dancer has to take her place at very short notice. In a ballet company, understudies are called "covers." The ballet staff will help the cover with coaching and a rehearsal, and all the other dancers will give as much support as they can.

Making light work
The lighting design, or plan, is programmed into a computer at a desk at the back of the auditorium (the audience area). Most lighting changes, called "cues," occur automatically, and are monitored by the lighting manager.

CREATING A SCENE

DESIGNERS USE color, texture, and lighting to transform the stage into an imaginary world. They work closely with the choreographer because they need to share the same ideas about how the ballet will finally look. Designs for costumes and scenery begin months before the first performance as rough sketches and models. Designers also need to be skilled architects and engineers because some stage sets are very complicated, with large pieces of scenery that are moved by machinery.

Paper flowers for the set of Alice in Wonderland

Making props
Props, such as these paper flowers, are specially made in workshops by skilled propmakers. Nothing is quite what it seems – a heavy jeweled drinking glass may be made of light plastic resin, for example. All props must be easy to handle on stage, durable, and safe.

Model set for English National Ballet's 1997 production of The Nutcracker.

Designing the set of The Nutcracker
Set designers train in theater design at art school. They must also understand how a stage works – how it can be rotated, or how levels can be changed. However stunning the designs, they will need to be moved around very quickly and quietly by the stage crew.

The scene for the Christmas Eve party

Clara's home
This set is for the party scene. The tiny model furniture will be copied by carpenters for the stage. The trimming around the proscenium arch (the frame of the stage) suggests Christmas presents and boxes of candy.

There must be room for the corps de ballet to dance.

Warm pink lighting creates a cotton-candy effect.

The Land of Snow
Clara dances with the Snowflakes in the Land of Snow. The lighting designer will use blue lighting and fake snowflakes to create a wintry scene.

The Kingdom of the Sugar Plum Fairy
Clara celebrates among the dancing sweets. This designer has created candy cane columns and dressed the dancers to look like licorice candies.

The Nutcracker Prince and the Ice Queen dance among the glistening Snowflakes in the Land of Snow.

DRESSING THE PART

Costumes give ballet its special magic. They are designed to show off the beautiful and dramatic movements and to create a character. But they also need to be practical and durable. They will be worn by many different dancers and packed into trunks and unpacked, or hung on racks when the company goes on tour. They must be easy to clean – dancers perspire – and while perhaps looking delicate, will need to survive being caught on scenery or other dancers' costumes. Above all, a costume should allow the dancer to move freely and feel comfortable.

Romantic tutus
Margot Fonteyn, above, in the longer style of tutu worn in Romantic ballets (see page 50). Her costume is from *Les Sylphides*, created by Fokine for Diaghilev. The costume design for this ballet has hardly changed since the first production in 1909.

Behind the mask
Masks such as these realistic catlike ones from *The Sleeping Beauty* add drama to a costume and help performers to dance in character. However, masks can be hard to dance in. For example, they make it more difficult for dancers to use their heads properly in *pirouettes* (see page 20).

The White Cat's furry mask is made from a lightweight material.

Sleeves are detached from the bodice to allow more movement.

Puss in Boots wears pawlike mittens.

Long, pointed fingernails are attached to gloves.

A magical outfit
Kostchei, the magician from *The Firebird*, wears a false nose, long fingernails, and a wig. The design for this costume was originally created by Serge Golovine.

All tutus are made of at least 14 layers of gathered net.

Male costumes
Male dancers usually wear tights so that they can move freely when performing difficult steps such as *grand allegro* and *batterie*. This costume is a stretchy unitard decorated with trimmings.

The croquet mallet is a prop, not a part of the costume.

A square cut turns a classical tutu into a playing card.

Fancy dress
A designer may take a traditional costume and adapt it for a modern ballet. This imaginative square tutu is worn in *Alice in Wonderland* by a croquet-playing card.

The classical tutu worn by the Sugar Plum Fairy in *The Nutcracker* adds to the enchanting atmosphere of her dance.

MAKING UP

DANCERS WEAR MAKEUP because strong stage lighting can make their faces look pale and uninteresting, and features may seem to disappear unless they are highlighted with makeup. Fantasy or grotesque characters need much heavier, theatrical makeup. Some makeup designs for characters in older ballets, such as for the puppet Petrushka (see page 46), are an important part of the costume design, and are handed down from dancer to dancer. Wigs and hairstyles also help to build a character.

Making of a dancer
The lights around a makeup mirror resemble strong stage lighting so dancers can see how their makeup will look when they are on stage.

Stage makeup
This is the makeup for a female dancer. It seems heavy, but will look more subtle on stage. Dancers learn how to apply makeup while training. They will spend about an hour doing their hair and makeup before a performance.

Eyelashes

Mascara

Dancers stick false eyelashes onto their eyelids with special glue.

Blusher

Apply darker blusher just below your cheekbones.

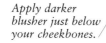

Lipsticks

Lightly brush a darker shading of blusher just below your jaw line.

1 Using a sponge, apply foundation all over your face and around your eyes in broad, sweeping movements. Gently brush loose translucent powder over the foundation.

Give eyebrows more shape and definition with an eyebrow pencil.

Brush highlighter gently over the eye socket.

Brush blusher across your hairline for definition.

2 Brush eye shadow over your eyelids. With an eyeliner pencil, draw a dark line above and below your eyes, close to the lashes.

Brush more highlighter under your eyebrows.

Eye shadow

Put darker shadow in the creases of your eyelids.

Use a brush to apply lipstick.

3 Brush your lashes with mascara. Apply blusher in a circular motion along your cheekbones. Use a lip pencil to outline your lips and fill them in with lipstick.

Creating Bluebird

The Bluebird is a fantasy character from *The Sleeping Beauty*. The designer has set this production of the ballet in the 18th century, so the Bluebird looks like a gentleman of that time. Blue glitter has been woven into his wig, and his makeup is blue and exaggerated.

The mesh base of the wig is barely visible.

Emphasize your eyebrows with an eyebrow pencil.

Black lines outline your eyes.

Put highlighter below your eyebrows.

Wigs are fitted after the makeup has been applied.

Foundation and powder stop your face from shining on stage.

1 Apply foundation and powder over your face. Paint black eyeliner on your upper and lower eyelids, close to your eyelashes. Then blend blue and gray shadow over your eyelids.

2 The mesh base of the wig is glued and placed squarely on your forehead, then pinned securely to your hair.

3 After the performance, you can remove the makeup with soap and water. To remove heavier makeup, use moisturizer and tissues or cotton wads. Alcohol dissolves the glue used to stick on wigs.

Foundation

Eyeliner

Face powder

Makeup supplies
For basic makeup, dancers use everyday cosmetics. Unusual foundation colors, greasepaint sticks, and special effects are sold in theatrical makeup stores.

Character makeup
These are characters from the ballet *Alice in Wonderland*, which is based on the Lewis Carroll story. As well as using colorful makeup, both are using a prosthesis (false body part) made of soft foam rubber – a false nose for the Caterpillar, and a half-mask for the Duchess. Each prosthesis is glued to the body, and blended in with makeup so that the place where they join is invisible.

The Duchess

The Caterpillar

Styling your hair

Hair must be styled close to the head and off the face, so as not to distract you or your partner. It is very unprofessional for hair to come loose while dancing.

Hair is parted in the center.

Sections are pinned here to lie flat.

This makes a good base for a headdress.

1 Brush your hair and divide it into three sections. Sweep the back section up into a ponytail.

2 Lifting the side sections, twist them and secure with barrettes on the top of your head, close to the ponytail.

3 Twist the ponytail around into a bun, and secure it with long hairpins and a hair net. Apply lots of hair spray to fix any stray wisps of hair.

CURTAIN UP!

AFTER MONTHS of hard work, the performance is about to begin. Dancers limber up in the wings and wait for their cue. Backstage, the crew makes sure that everything is ready and all the props are on hand. In the auditorium, the lights dim and the audience chatter fades to silence as the conductor lifts his baton and the orchestra plays the first bars of the overture. At last, the curtain goes up and the stage comes to life with movement and light.

Final touches
Dancers apply their stage makeup before their wigs and costumes. Ballet companies have specially trained makeup supervisors to give advice. The supervisors will also watch performance rehearsals to make sure the makeup has the right effect.

Dancers prepare several pairs of shoes before each performance.

Trained staff helps the performers to put on wigs.

Hair designs
Wigs and hairstyles are part of costume design. A big production needs many different wigs, which must be regularly cleaned and restyled. Wigs are made up separately by wig-makers, and maintained by a specially trained staff, which also advises on hairstyles for dancers not wearing wigs.

Sticky shoes
Some stages can be slippery, so dancers use a sticky, white powder called rosin to prevent them from slipping while they are performing. Before they go on stage, the dancers rub their feet in the wooden rosin box kept in the wings. Rosin may also be used inside the shoes to help keep them on.

Curtain call
There are two kinds of curtain calls: one within the stage set for all the dancers, the other in front of the curtain for the principals. Dancers may be presented with bouquets of flowers, and the choreographer, composer, and designer also join the principals on stage on the first night, or *première*.

In the opening scene of *The Nutcracker*, Clara dances delightedly with her Nutcracker Doll.

DANCING TO MUSIC

WHEN MUSIC COMBINES with dancing, costumes, and scenery, it creates a spellbinding spectacle. In making a new ballet, choreographers can either use music that already exists, or they can ask a composer to write new music. The composer and the choreographer then work as a team to make the choreographer's dream a reality. The music helps the choreographer express his ideas clearly through the dancers. Music and movement work together to convey ideas and emotions.

Court composer
Jean-Baptiste Lully (1632–87) composed some of the first ballet music, at the court of Louis XIV of France. Lully came to the court as a dancer and appeared with the King in several ballets, for which he composed some of the music. He became a favorite of the King's and went on to head the Académie de Musique. Lully is best known for *Le Ballet de la nuit* (1653), in which Louis XIV appeared as the Rising Sun (see page 48), and *Le Triomphe de l'amour* (1681). Both productions were a mixture of dance and opera.

The orchestra
Ballet music may be composed for a few musicians, or for a full symphony orchestra led by a conductor. It can be in any style, from classical to rock. Some compositions are electroacoustic, or prerecorded. With live music, the relationship between dancers and musicians is very important. They must also work as a team.

Frédéric Chopin (1810–49)
Polish-born composer Frédéric Chopin was never commissioned to write ballet music, but his pieces have often been used for ballets. The best-known of these is *Chopiniana*, later known as *Les Sylphides*, which used his delightful piano pieces. Other choreographers who have used his music include Jerome Robbins in *The Concert* (1956) and *Dances at a Gathering* (1969), and Sir Frederick Ashton for his ballet *A Month in the Country* (1976).

Léo Delibes (1836–91)
Using a *leitmotif* (a musical theme for each character) for the ballet *Coppélia*, French-born Léo Delibes brought new life to ballet music. The music tells the story so clearly that you can almost see the ballet in your imagination as you listen.

Igor Stravinsky

Nijinsky in his costume for Petrushka

Pyotr Tchaikovsky (1840–93)

Tchaikovsky's scores for *Swan Lake*, *The Sleeping Beauty*, and *The Nutcracker* were specially commissioned by choreographer Marius Petipa. Petipa gave strict instructions about how much music he wanted and how it had to sound. Tchaikovsky and Petipa were an extremely successful composer-choreographer partnership.

Serge Prokofiev (1891–1953)

Born in Russia, Serge Prokofiev wrote music for the Ballets Russes and the Bolshoi Ballet. In the United States, Prokofiev's wonderful scores for both *Romeo and Juliet* (1938) and *Cinderella* (1945) took ballet music to new dramatic heights. Both ballets are danced today in many different productions. His composition *Peter and the Wolf*, written to introduce children to orchestral music, has also been used to create ballets. Prokofiev wrote opera and other classical forms of music, as well as music for films.

Composer Carl Davis (left) at a rehearsal for Alice in Wonderland *with Derek Deane (right), Artistic Director of English National Ballet*

The score, or musical notation

Igor Stravinsky (1882–1971)

Russian-born Igor Stravinsky wrote the music for *The Firebird*, *Petrushka*, and *Les Noces* for Diaghilev's Ballets Russes. Audiences were sometimes shocked by Stravinsky's music, especially *Rite of Spring*, choreographed by Vaslav Nijinsky, which looked and sounded very different from other ballets. After moving to the US, Stravinsky wrote *Duo Concertant* and *Apollo* for the New York City Ballet, and music for many other ballets.

Carl Davis

In 1997, the Director of English National Ballet, Derek Deane, asked Carl Davis to compose the music for a new ballet, *Alice in Wonderland*. The composer usually attends rehearsals and may make changes to the music at this stage.

STEP BY STEP

THERE ARE MANY DIFFERENT KINDS of ballet. Some tell a story, others develop a theme, and a few are simply about dancing for its own sake (abstract ballets). In any ballet, the role of the choreographer is to decide how he or she will present the ballet and what steps the dancers should perform. Progress can be slow. The choreographer begins work with the dancers and just one minute of dancing can take an hour to create. The dancers help by showing the choreographer what they think he or she wants, which can spark other creative ideas.

Right hand in front of the body, wrist facing down

Dame Ninette celebrating her birthday at the Royal Opera House, together with dancers from The Royal Ballet

Ninette de Valois (born 1898)
Dame Ninette de Valois has choreographed wonderfully dramatic ballets – *Checkmate*, *The Rake's Progress*, and *Job*. As well as being a choreographer, Dame Ninette is the founder of The Royal Ballet and the Royal Ballet School and is a great teacher. She encouraged John Cranko, Ashton, Bintley, and MacMillan to become choreographers.

Frederick Ashton (1906–88)
One of the greatest choreographers of the 20th century, Ashton created many ballets for The Royal Ballet. They included ballets based on stories such as *Cinderella* and *Tales of Beatrix Potter*, love stories like *A Month in the Country*, and abstract ballets such as *Symphonic Variations*.

Balanchine demonstrates the steps in the studio.

The dancer watches in the mirror before repeating the movement.

George Balanchine (1904–83)
This legendary choreographer was born in St. Petersburg, Russia, and joined Diaghilev's Ballets Russes. He was cofounder, with Lincoln Kirstein, of the world-famous New York City Ballet. His ballets, such as *Stars and Stripes* and *Jewels,* are mostly abstract, allowing dancers to show dazzling technique and musicality. His other ballets, such as *Serenade* and his neoclassical masterpieces *Agon* and *Apollo*, create mood and atmosphere.

Legs in "splits" in the air, with the right foot in front and the left foot behind

Kenneth MacMillan (1929–92)

A great choreographer who worked mostly with The Royal Ballet, MacMillan's works range from abstract ballets such as *Song of the Earth* to his moving narrative ballet based on Shakespeare's *Romeo and Juliet*. MacMillan is particularly well known for his spectacular dramatic ballets such as *Mayerling*, *Manon*, and *Anastasia*.

David Bintley (born 1957)

British choreographer Bintley trained at the Royal Ballet School and joined Sadler's Wells Ballet as a dancer. He is now Artistic Director of Birmingham Royal Ballet. His abstract ballets are modern ballet at its best, and he has also presented fairy tales such as *The Snow Queen* and story-ballets such as *Hobson's Choice*.

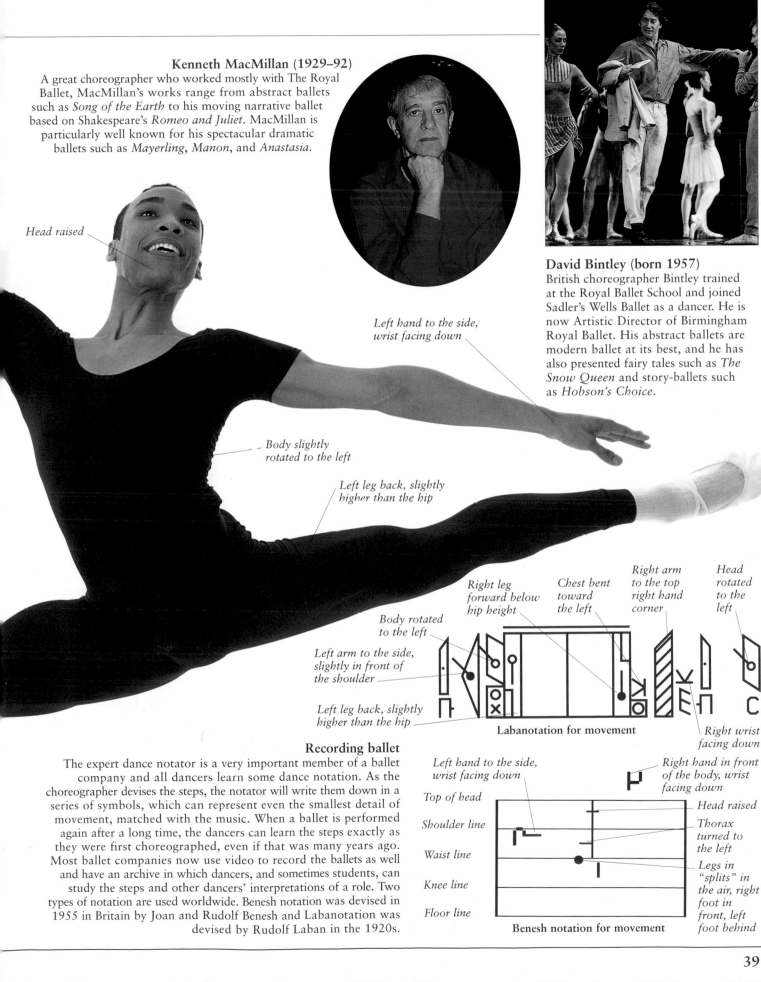

Head raised

Left hand to the side, wrist facing down

Body slightly rotated to the left

Left leg back, slightly higher than the hip

Right leg forward below hip height

Chest bent toward the left

Right arm to the top right hand corner

Head rotated to the left

Body rotated to the left

Left arm to the side, slightly in front of the shoulder

Left leg back, slightly higher than the hip

Labanotation for movement

Right wrist facing down

Left hand to the side, wrist facing down

Right hand in front of the body, wrist facing down

Top of head

Shoulder line

Waist line

Knee line

Floor line

Head raised

Thorax turned to the left

Legs in "splits" in the air, right foot in front, left foot behind

Benesh notation for movement

Recording ballet

The expert dance notator is a very important member of a ballet company and all dancers learn some dance notation. As the choreographer devises the steps, the notator will write them down in a series of symbols, which can represent even the smallest detail of movement, matched with the music. When a ballet is performed again after a long time, the dancers can learn the steps exactly as they were first choreographed, even if that was many years ago. Most ballet companies now use video to record the ballets as well and have an archive in which dancers, and sometimes students, can study the steps and other dancers' interpretations of a role. Two types of notation are used worldwide. Benesh notation was devised in 1955 in Britain by Joan and Rudolf Benesh and Labanotation was devised by Rudolf Laban in the 1920s.

39

BALLET STARS

A PRINCIPAL DANCER CAN TRAVEL the world, dancing as a guest artist with other ballet companies, or can stay with one company. While performing the same steps in a ballet, each dancer will bring his or her own personality to the role. This is known as the interpretation. A dancer's career is quite short, but very demanding. Although many stop performing in their late thirties, they often stay in the world of ballet as teachers, choreographers, or notators. Principal dancers can become artistic directors of companies, where they use their experience to lead a company, encourage choreographers, and develop younger dancers.

Natalia Makarova
Born in Leningrad, Makarova became a dancer with the Kirov Ballet. In 1970, she decided to stay in the West. She is famous for her interpretations of *Giselle* and *Swan Lake*. Makarova has also helped ballet companies mount productions of classical ballets.

Irek Mukhamedov
Mukhamedov trained at the Bolshoi Ballet School and was a principal dancer with the company. In 1990, he joined The Royal Ballet. A great actor as well as a superb dancer, he has created many new roles in modern ballets. Mukhamedov has also directed and performed with his own company, taking ballet to new audiences.

The costume suggests a Roman tunic.

Mukhamedov in the dramatic role Spartacus

Margot Fonteyn
Fonteyn was born in 1919 and became a soloist with the Sadler's Wells Ballet when she was just 16. She died in 1991, but will always be remembered for her beauty and elegance as an international ballerina. She is famous for her interpretation of Ashton's *Ondine* and *Symphonic Variations* and MacMillan's *Romeo and Juliet*, as well as the classical roles.

Fonteyn as the exotic Firebird

Fonteyn's partner in The Firebird *was Michael Somes.*

This costume was designed by Bakst (see page 54).

Mikhail Baryshnikov

One of the greatest male dancers of today, Baryshnikov began his career as a dancer with the Kirov Ballet. He moved to the West in 1974. As well as dancing and directing, Baryshnikov has also acted in films and extended his own technique by working with many different choreographers and dance styles. He currently directs and performs with his own company, The White Oak Dance Project.

Darcey Bussell as Princess Aurora in The Sleeping Beauty

Baryshnikov dances in Le Spectre de la rose, *in a role first created by Nijinsky (see page 42).*

Darcey is wearing a classical tutu.

Sylvie Guillem dances in the role of Cinderella.

Darcey Bussell

Bussell was born in London in 1969. She trained at the Royal Ballet School and has been a principal dancer with The Royal Ballet since 1989. Her fresh and youthful approach to roles, and her virtuoso technique, have made her one of Britain's favorite and most famous dancers. Bussell has appeared as a guest artist with the New York City Ballet and in Russia, where audiences were delighted by her interpretations of classical ballet.

Sylvie Guillem

Trained at the Paris Opéra Ballet School, Guillem later joined the company before leaving to become principal artist with The Royal Ballet. Guillem has amazing technique and extension and has inspired choreographers to make ballets that use her technical abilities to the full. She is seen here in a French production of *Cinderella*.

DANCE PARTNERS

Wʜᴇɴ ᴍᴀᴋɪɴɢ ᴀ ɴᴇᴡ ʙᴀʟʟᴇᴛ, choreographers look for principal dancers who have a particular magic, a way of dancing together and communicating with the audience that will make the ballet powerful and memorable. These special partnerships happen with two dancers whose technique, personality, and body shape are in harmony with each other. This in turn can inspire the choreographer to create ballets that show the dancers at their best and make them popular with audiences. Here are just a few of the many famous partnerships throughout history.

Nijinsky and Karsavina

Vaslav Nijinsky and Tamara Karsavina were Russian-born dancers who trained at the Imperial Ballet School in St. Petersburg. They were members of Diaghilev's Ballets Russes and danced together in several ballets choreographed by Michel Fokine. This picture is from *Le Spectre de la rose*. Nijinsky and Karsavina created a dream-like quality in this ballet.

Karsavina was famous for her beautiful movements and expressive face.

Real pigeons are used to represent the couple.

Sibley and Dowell

Antoinette Sibley and Anthony Dowell trained at the Royal Ballet School and were principal dancers with The Royal Ballet. They created many roles for Sir Frederick Ashton. Their fine technique and lyrical style is captured here in this picture from *The Dream*, in which they played Oberon and Titania. Sir Anthony Dowell is now the Artistic Director of The Royal Ballet.

Baryshnikov and Makarova

Natalia Makarova left the Kirov Ballet in 1970 and in 1974, Mikhail Baryshnikov also left. Both went on to dance in the US and Europe. They first danced together in American Ballet Theatre, where their dazzling technique made them ideal partners. They went on to dance as principal guest artists with different partners in many other companies. Here they are Basilio and Kitri dancing the virtuoso *pas de deux* from Petipa's *Don Quixote* (see page 45).

These costumes reflect the Spanish setting of the ballet.

Seymour and Gable

Lynn Seymour and Christopher Gable both trained at the Royal Ballet School. Sir Kenneth MacMillan chose them for several of his dramatic ballets, such as *The Invitation*. Both were gifted dancers as well as fine actors, and had a passion that enthralled audiences. This picture is from Ashton's *The Two Pigeons*, in which, after many arguments, two young lovers are finally reunited.

Farrell and Martins

Suzanne Farrell and Peter Martins danced with the New York City Ballet. Farrell created roles for Balanchine that showed her beautiful leg extension and immaculate technique. An ideal Balanchine partnership, Farrell and Martins perfectly expressed the energy and virtuosity of his choreography. Martins is currently Ballet Master in Chief at the New York City Ballet.

Fonteyn and Nureyev

In 1961, a young Russian dancer called Rudolf Nureyev dramatically left Russia to dance in the West. The electricity in the partnership between him and Dame Margot Fonteyn became legendary. They created roles in ballets for Maurice Béjart, the experimental French choreographer, Ashton, and MacMillan, among other choreographers. In rehearsal and on stage, they seemed to bring something fresh and exciting to the choreography, which inspired all the other dancers.

Marguerite and Armand *was choreographed for Fonteyn and Nureyev by Frederick Ashton in 1963. It is a tragic love story set in Paris in the 19th century.*

TELLING TALES

NARRATIVE BALLETS tell a story. They usually take the form of several short scenes, called "acts," separated by an intermission. Small group dances, *pas de deux*, and solos help to create the atmosphere, while the story is told with acting and mime in larger crowd scenes. Sometimes there will be a display of dancing, called a *divertissement*, which does not tell the story, but presents virtuoso, or highly skilled, dancing for its own sake. At the end of the ballet there may be a group scene, called a "tableau," on which the curtain will fall.

Giselle
Choreography: Coralli and Perrot (1841) *Music*: Adam
Giselle is a village girl who loves to dance. She meets Prince Albrecht, who is disguised as a villager. When a royal hunting party arrives, the Princess recognizes Albrecht and tells the villagers they are to be married. Giselle is distraught at Albrecht's betrayal and dies in her mother's arms. At night, Albrecht visits Giselle's grave. He meets the Wilis, the spirits of girls who loved to dance and were betrayed by men. Their Queen, Myrtha, orders Albrecht to dance until he dies. Giselle still loves Albrecht and dances with him. At dawn, he is saved, as the Wilis and Giselle return to their graves.

Swanilda pretends to be Coppélia and dances with stiff, jerky movements like a doll.

Dr. Coppélius can't believe his eyes as Coppélia seems to come to life.

Coppélia
Choreography: Saint-Léon (1870) *Music*: Delibes
Franz and Swanilda are sweethearts, but Franz is fascinated by Coppélia, a doll made by Dr. Coppélius. Swanilda and her friends creep into the doll workshop. When Dr. Coppélius suddenly returns, Swanilda dresses in Coppélia's clothes and hides. Franz comes to find Coppélia. Dr. Coppélius seizes him and transfers Franz's spirit to the doll. Swanilda pretends to be the doll coming to life and performs lively dances. Franz awakes and they run out, leaving a heartbroken Dr. Coppélius. Swanilda and Franz dance a *pas de deux* at their wedding, and she apologizes to Dr. Coppélius.

Aurora falls asleep after pricking her finger on the spindle.

Everyone looks on in dismay as the Queen cradles Aurora.

The Sleeping Beauty

Choreography: Petipa (1890) *Music*: Tchaikovsky
Dancing fairies bring gifts to Princess Aurora's christening. The wicked fairy Carabosse arrives uninvited and says in a mime sequence that when Aurora is 16, she will prick her finger on a spindle and die. The Lilac Fairy says Aurora will only sleep and reawaken when a Prince kisses her. On her birthday, Aurora dances the Rose Adagio with four suitors, then pricks her finger. Helped by the Lilac Fairy, the Prince awakens Aurora, and they celebrate their marriage with a grand *pas de deux*.

Kitri uses a Spanish fan to flirt with Basilio.

Don Quixote

Choreography: Petipa (1869) *Music*: Minkus
This ballet is set in Spain. Don Quixote is an old man who dreams of being a Knight and he seeks adventure with his servant Sancho Panza. Kitri is a beautiful girl in love with Basilio, but her father, Lorenzo, wants her to marry wealthy Gamache. After many adventures, Kitri and Basilio finally do marry. At their wedding celebration, the lovers dance a famous *pas de deux*, which has virtuoso solos for both Kitri and Basilio and ends with an exciting *coda*. Don Quixote and his servant then leave for more adventures.

Basilio serenades Kitri with a Spanish guitar.

Swan Lake

Choreography: Petipa and Ivanov (1895)
Music: Tchaikovsky
It is Prince Siegfried's birthday. His mother tells him he must soon marry, but he prefers to hunt by the lake. Swans fly over and he takes aim – but they become beautiful women as they land. Siegfried falls in love with Odette, the Swan Princess. She tells him in a mime sequence that the evil magician Rothbart has turned her and her friends into swans. At a ball, Rothbart and his daughter Odile arrive. Odile is in black, disguised as Odette. Siegfried is delighted. They dance a *pas de deux* and he vows to marry her. A vision of a weeping Odette appears, and Siegfried realizes he has been deceived. At the lake, the swans dance sadly. Siegfried appears and he and Odette triumph over Rothbart with their love.

The swans are fearful of the huntsmen by the lake.

MORE STORYTELLING

Some ballets, such as *Swan Lake*, use original choreography, but entirely new scenery and costumes. In others, such as *Romeo and Juliet*, the story stays the same but is presented in a variety of versions, each with its own choreography, scenery, and costumes. The choreography, scenery, and music are very closely linked in ballets such as *Petrushka*, which are so much a part of ballet history that new productions are made to look as much like the original as possible. Choreographers may also update traditional ballets with contemporary choreography.

The Snowflakes dance in the Land of Snow.

The Firebird flutters her hands to suggest birdlike movements.

The Firebird
Choreography: Fokine (1910) *Music*: Stravinsky
A princess and her friends dance in an enchanted garden, where they have been imprisoned by the magician Kostchei. Prince Ivan climbs into the garden and captures a firebird, who flutters wildly and tries to escape. She gives Ivan one of her feathers in exchange for her freedom, but says she will return to help him if he is in danger. As Ivan watches the Princess and her friends shaking golden apples from the trees, he is captured by Kostchei and his creatures. The Firebird returns as promised, and shows Ivan how to destroy Kostchei by breaking a giant egg containing his soul. The spell broken, all the hideous creatures imprisoned by the magician are released. Ivan and the Princess marry and are crowned King and Queen.

The Nutcracker
Choreography: Ivanov (1892) *Music*: Tchaikovsky
Clara is given a Nutcracker doll at a Christmas Eve party. After the party, Clara creeps downstairs, falls asleep, and dreams that giant rats and mice fight with her new doll. Clara saves him and he turns into a Prince. He takes her on a magical trip to the Land of Snow and the Kingdom of Sweets. Clara is entertained by a *divertissement* of dancing sweets and a *pas de deux* for the Sugar Plum Fairy and Nutcracker Prince. She wakes up back home.

Petrushka
Choreography: Fokine (1911) *Music*: Stravinsky
At Butterweek Fair in St. Petersburg, Russia, a Showman presents three puppets: the Moor, the Ballerina, and sad Petrushka. After the show, the puppets squabble and Petrushka dances a tragic solo to show how much he loves the Ballerina. The Moor chases Petrushka out of the booth and strikes him with his scimitar. To the horror of the crowd, Petrushka seems to bleed, but the Showman lifts up his body and shows it is only a puppet, leaking sawdust. As night falls and the fairground closes, the ghost of Petrushka rises above the sideshow, taunting the Showman.

Colas kneels to kiss Lise's hand while her friends gather around at the harvest.

La Fille mal gardée
Choreography: Ashton (1960) *Music*: Herold
Lise and her mother, Widow Simone, live on a farm. Lise is in love with Colas, a neighbor. Widow Simone introduces Lise to Alain, the son of a wealthy local farmer, but Lise prefers Colas. At the harvest celebrations, Widow Simone dances a comical clog dance and the villagers celebrate with a Maypole dance. Back home, Lise uses mime to daydream about marrying Colas. Colas suddenly jumps out of the corn sheaves. He has heard every word! Widow Simone finally agrees to let Lise and Colas marry and they dance a joyful *pas de deux* to show that everything has ended well.

Juliet despairs when she awakes to find Romeo dead in the tomb beside her.

Romeo and Juliet
Choreography: MacMillan (1965) *Music*: Prokofiev
Based on Shakespeare's play, this ballet is about two young lovers whose families hate one another. Romeo and Juliet meet at a ball and dance a beautiful *pas de deux* beneath Juliet's balcony. A priest secretly marries them. Juliet's cousin, Tybalt, kills Romeo's best friend, Mercutio, in a fight. Romeo retaliates and is sent away. Juliet's parents arrange for her to marry Paris, but Juliet takes a potion. Her friends dance in with her wedding dress and think she is dead. Romeo rushes to her tomb and takes poison just as Juliet wakes. Grief-stricken, Juliet stabs herself.

BALLET BEGINNINGS

BALLET BEGAN IN ITALY in the 15th century and the word ballet comes from the Italian word *ballo*, meaning "dance." Ballet was taken to France from Italy by Catherine de Medici, and developed at the French courts of the 16th century. It was a part of court entertainment – grand spectacles with scenery and costumes, which included speeches, processions, music, and dancing. The first performance of ballet on stage in theaters was in 1669, when it was presented as a part of an opera.

The Triumph of Love
This is the program for Beauchamp's ballet, *The Triumph of Love*, performed on stage at the Paris Opéra in 1681.

Louis XIV as the Rising Sun in Le Ballet de la nuit, *performed at Versailles in 1653*

Magnificent headdress suggests the Sun's rays.

Posture is similar to that of today's dancers.

An early ballet
Ballet comique de la reine was performed on October 15, 1581. It was created by Balthasar de Beaujoyeux for a wedding celebration, and was a mixture of recitation, singing, and dancing. Watched by 10,000 people, the ballet showed scenes from Greek and Roman mythology, and lasted six hours.

Hands and fingers are poised in positions still used in ballet.

Louis XIV
The magnificent Sun King, Louis XIV, loved dancing and took part in his first ballet when he was 13. He and his dancing master, Pierre Beauchamp, set up the Académie Royale de Danse, where the five basic positions (see page 12) were written down for the first time. French is still the language of ballet today.

Legs are turned out to show off calves and ankles.

Courtly manners
Dancing was as much a part of courtly life as riding and good manners, and dancers in early ballets were therefore not professionals. Women were allowed to dance at court, in solos, and in groups, but were not allowed to perform on stage until *Le Triomphe de l'amour* was produced in 1681.

Softer hair style replaces wigs, allowing more movement.

Both dancers wear lighter shoes.

Ballet with a story

One of the first people to make ballet more natural and expressive, without heavy costumes and masks, was the 18th-century choreographer Jean-Georges Noverre. This form was called *ballet d'action* and it was designed to tell a story. The Italian version was called *coreodramma*, and this picture shows Salvatore Vigano and his wife Maria de Medina wearing lighter costumes.

Auguste Vestris

Ballet used the lively steps and patterns of folk dances, as well as elaborate court postures. Auguste Vestris, above, was one of the star dancers of the late 18th century. He delighted audiences with very high jumps, turns, and beating steps.

A daring display

A famous ballerina of the 18th century, Marie Camargo, above, began as a dancer in the *corps de ballet* of the Paris Opéra. One day, when a male dancer failed to turn up for a show, Marie took his place and brilliantly invented the steps. She raised the hem of her elaborate costume to reveal her ankles and enable her to perform more difficult steps, such as jumps and beats, despite wearing shoes with heels.

ROMANTIC ERA

MANY OF THE FEATURES of ballet today began in the 19th century, in the Romantic era. Great developments were taking place in science and industry, and it seemed that the more people found out about the real world, the more they escaped into fantasy in books, music, art, and ballet. Female dancers had more important roles than the males. Ballerinas wore softly gathered skirts, rose on tiptoe in specially stiffened shoes, and pretended to be fairies, sylphs, and other exotic beings.

Carlotta Grisi
Giselle was created by Jules Perrot in 1841 for Carlotta Grisi, a famous ballerina of the time. The story was written by Théophile Gautier, one of her admirers. Here, Grisi wears a softly gathered calf-length dress, adapted from the ball gowns of the time. In this scene, Giselle has become a spirit and dances in a clearing in the forest.

Carlo Blasis
Born in Italy, Blasis was the most important teacher of the 19th century. He taught famous dancers all over Europe, and wrote several books, outlining his thoughts on teaching and performing ballet. His ideas form the basis of contemporary ballet styles.

Marie Taglioni dancing in Zéphire et Flore

On tiptoe
Marie Taglioni was the first ballerina to dance on the tips of her toes. Taught by her father, Filippo Taglioni, she was known for her delicacy, grace, and effortless dancing, especially in *La Sylphide* (1832). Her choice of white costumes, repeated in *Les Sylphides* (1909), as well as her dancing on *pointe*, inspired many Romantic ballets and dancers.

Headdresses were made from circles of flowers.

Softly tied-back hairstyles were fashionable.

Arms curve softly in true Romantic style.

The Three Graces
A short ballet by Jules Perrot, called *The Judgement of Paris*, brought together three famous ballerinas of the time: Marie Taglioni, Lucile Grahn, and Fanny Cerrito. Also famous during this time was Fanny Elssler, well known for dancing an exciting Spanish dance called the *Cachucha*. An adoring public treated these ballerinas like stars.

Soft satin ballet shoes were lightly darned.

Lucile Grahn
This picture of Lucile Grahn as Eoline the Dryad (woodland sprite) is from 1845 and captures the atmosphere of the era. That same year, Jules Perrot brought Grisi, Taglioni, and Grahn together with Fanny Cerrito, and choreographed the famous *Pas de quatre*.

Giselle
Romantic ballet choreographers liked to use folk themes, as suggested by Giselle's embroidered apron over her tutu.
One of the few Romantic ballets still performed today, Giselle's costume remains similar to its original design.

CLASSICAL STYLE

THE END OF THE 19TH CENTURY was a splendid time for ballet. The Classical ballets, which still form the basis of the repertoire for many companies, were choreographed in Russia by Frenchman Marius Petipa. Petipa became ballet master of the Imperial Russian Ballet in 1862 and he created a formal structure for the ballets, which celebrated the technical ability of dancers. He also took the developments made in ballet technique during the Romantic era – dancing on *pointe*, and a greater variety of gravity-defying jumps – even further.

Skirt is longer than present-day tutus.

Faroukh Ruzimatov of the Kirov Ballet dancing in Le Corsaire

Classical ballet
Marius Petipa's Classical ballets contain a mixture of storytelling through dance and mime, and dance for its own sake. They include *Swan Lake*, *The Nutcracker*, and *The Sleeping Beauty*. Petipa choreographed the latter in 1890 at the Maryinsky Theater in St. Petersburg. It is a perfect example of a 19th-century ballet, with its mixture of formal dance patterns for the *corps de ballet*, virtuoso solos, and *pas de deux*.

Male virtuosity
Male dancers played a much more prominent role in late 19th-century ballets than they had earlier in the Romantic era. Classical ballet style introduced flamboyant leaps and the convention of ending male solos with a series of dazzling turns.

The Dying Swan
One of the world's greatest ballerinas, Anna Pavlova, trained at the Imperial Ballet Academy in Russia. She delighted thousands worldwide with her poignant solo performance of the Dying Swan, created by Michel Fokine in 1907. Resisting modern developments, Pavlova's dancing remained true to the Classical style.

Birmingham Royal Ballet's production of *The Nutcracker*

Character dancing

The 1870 ballet, *Coppélia*, created a link between the Romantic and Classical styles. Choreography and music were closely woven together, and different musical themes were used to represent each character. *Coppélia* was a more realistic story about everyday people. Arthur Saint-Léon, its choreographer, used folk dances from many countries, such as Spain and Hungary.

Swanilda dancing in Spanish style

The male dancer's position is in harmony with the ballerina.

A shorter tutu makes this type of position much easier.

Pas de deux

Marius Petipa introduced a format for the *pas de deux* in his ballets, which made them much more interesting and demanding. The emphasis was still largely on the female dancer's skills, but solos for both partners gave male and female dancers the opportunity to show off their technique. The *pas de deux* ends with a dazzling display of virtuoso (highly skilled) dancing, called a *coda*.

This fish dive is from The Sleeping Beauty.

A central group of soloists with the corps de ballet placed at the side is typical of ballets in this style.

MODERN MOVEMENT

Ballet in the 20th century experienced enormous change, brought about by events such as the Russian Revolution, two World Wars, and the emancipation of women. These events also affected the arts. Ballet went on developing and absorbing different influences until it eventually spread worldwide. Some of the teachers and choreographers who made the most impact emerged from the Imperial Russian tradition. They kept the purity of the technique of classical ballet, but used it more dramatically.

Isadora Duncan
Michel Fokine saw Isadora dance in Russia in 1904. Although she was never part of the modern ballet movement, her unusually free way of dancing – unrestricted by *pointe* shoes and stiff costumes – may have made an impact on ballet choreographers.

Isadora danced barefoot in flowing costumes.

Bakst designs
One of the most celebrated designers of the Ballets Russes was Leon Bakst. He created a costume for *L'Après-midi d'un faune* made of an all-over body suit combined with makeup. Bakst was famous for his glowing colors and use of richly exotic fabrics, which influenced the fashion designers of the time. His drawings were works of art in themselves.

Nijinsky choreographed L'Après-midi d'un faune *and danced the rôle of a faun in it.*

Ballets Russes
Russian-born Sergei Diaghilev formed the Ballets Russes, which created a sensation in Paris in 1909. Diaghilev brought together composers, designers, and choreographers to create ballets that shocked and delighted audiences with their vivid colors, exotic glamor, and dazzling technique. Painters such as Pablo Picasso, and composers such as Igor Stravinsky, helped to make the ballets. By employing teachers who had begun at the Imperial Ballet, Diaghilev ensured that technique was properly taught.

An innovative choreographer
Michel Fokine created some of the best-loved ballets of the 20th century. After Fokine created *Les Sylphides* for the Imperial Russian Ballet, Sergei Diaghilev invited him to join the Ballets Russes. Fokine then choreographed *The Firebird* and *Petrushka,* ballets that tell magical stories in a fluid, dramatic way, and which changed the formal presentation of classical ballet forever.

Set design for Petrushka *by Alexander Benois*

A supported arabesque *in the modern style*

The dancers' costumes look like practice clothes, which is a feature of some Balanchine ballets.

Lise dances joyfully with a ribbon.

La Fille mal gardée

This ballet was first seen in the 18th century and was produced again in the Romantic era. In 1960, it was recrafted by Sir Frederick Ashton, who gave it a modern interpretation. Ashton uses classical ballet technique with English folk dance steps, and some charming mime, to create an up-to-date story ballet, loved by audiences for its warmth and humor.

Balanchine's ballets

Russian-born George Balanchine danced and choreographed for Diaghilev, before founding New York City Ballet. Firmly rooted in the classical tradition, he created ballets such as *Agon* (above), which use the traditional format of solo, *pas de deux*, and *corps de ballet* dancing. His ballets are dazzling presentations of classical ballet technique, which appear totally modern.

The Kirov Ballet's production *of* Romeo and Juliet

Romeo and Juliet

Many choreographers have devised ballets based on Shakespeare's *Romeo and Juliet*. The dramatic and emotional content of the story meant that ballet techniques, such as the *pas de deux*, had to become more expressive and athletic, with male and female dancers playing an equal part.

Abstract ballet

In the middle somewhat elevated was created by American William Forsythe in 1988. Although danced on *pointe*, the ballet uses contemporary features such as turned-in feet. There is no particular story or theme, but the ballet pushes the dancers to athletic extremes of extension and elevation.

WORLD OF BALLET

Every ballet company has its own style and character. The oldest ballet companies are the Paris Opéra Ballet, the Kirov, the Bolshoi, and the Royal Danish. In addition to those mentioned here, there are also ballet companies across Europe, South Africa, South America, the Far East, and Australasia. Most companies set up their own schools attached to the company, so that dancers can learn the company's particular style of dancing. Ballet companies not only establish traditions, but also exchange ideas with each other. There is constant movement of dancers, guest artists, and choreographers between companies and each brings a new and different interpretation of a production.

The Soldier's Tale

National Ballet of Canada
Based in Toronto, this company was founded in 1951 and produces new works as well as the classical ballets. Its first director was former Sadler's Wells ballerina Celia Franca.

The Bolshoi Ballet
Based at the Bolshoi Theater in Moscow since 1856, this company is famous for its dramatic, flamboyant style. The Bolshoi Ballet danced the very first performances of *Swan Lake* and *Don Quixote* and has trained many fine dancers. Its best-known ballerina was Galina Ulanova.

1986 production of Ivan the Terrible

American Ballet Theatre
Lucia Chase and Richard Pleasant formed this company, which was originally called the Ballet Theatre, in 1939. It later became American Ballet Theatre, based in New York, and is one of the cornerstones of American ballet, with many famous directors and dancers.

Paris Opéra's 1994 production of Swan Lake

Paris Opéra Ballet
One of the oldest companies, the Paris Opéra Ballet developed from the Académie Royale de Danse founded by Louis XIV in 1661. Many key figures in ballet history have made their début with the Paris Opéra, including Marie Taglioni and Fanny Elssler. Marius Petipa was ballet master in 1860; Rudolf Nureyev was Artistic Director 1983 to 1989.

A production of Toccato E Due Canzoni *by the Dance Theatre of Harlem*

Other companies

Birmingham Royal Ballet

This company grew out of The Royal Ballet's touring section. Under Sir Peter Wright's direction, they moved to the Birmingham Hippodrome in 1990. David Bintley is now Artistic Director.

The Kirov Ballet

Marius Petipa produced ballets such as *The Sleeping Beauty*, *The Nutcracker*, and *Raymonda* for this company, which was founded in St. Petersburg, Russia, in 1783. Its legendary school trained dancers such as Pavlova, Nijinsky, and Karsavina.

New York City Ballet

Ballets by its founder, George Balanchine, are central to this company's repertoire. Famous dancers, such as Jacques d'Amboise, have gone on to found or direct other American companies.

Dance Theatre of Harlem

Arthur Mitchell and Karel Shook founded this company to create more opportunities for black ballet dancers. It began as a school and its first professional performance was at the Guggenheim Museum in New York in 1971. The company performs classical and new works.

In this scene from Australian Ballet's production of Giselle, *Giselle knows that Albrecht has deceived her and she is distraught.*

Australian Ballet

Founded in 1962, the Australian Ballet presents all the major classical ballets, as well as specially commissioned new works. A number of dancers from the Royal Ballet helped to establish this company in its early years and its first Artistic Director was Peggy van Praagh, who had assisted Dame Ninette de Valois at the Sadler's Wells Royal Ballet.

The Royal Ballet

Founded by Dame Ninette de Valois, this company developed from the Sadler's Wells Ballet School based at Sadler's Wells Theatre in the 1930s. It became The Royal Ballet in 1956 and has two schools connected with it – the Lower School at White Lodge and the Upper School in West London. Since de Valois, the company has had many famous directors: Sir Frederick Ashton, Sir Kenneth MacMillan, and Norman Morrice. The current director is Sir Anthony Dowell.

American Ballet Theatre's 1990 production of Gaîté Parisienne

The Royal Ballet's production of The Sleeping Beauty

Glossary

Act
A section of a ballet. Ballets can be from one to four acts, with a break between acts called an intermission.

Adagio
Slow and sustained movements that require balance and control.

Alignment
The relationship of one part of the body to another, or the whole body to the space around it.

Allegro
Jumping and traveling steps, including *petit allegro*, which are small and fast, and *grand allegro*, which are larger movements.

Allongé
Extended or outstretched, as in hands or an *arabesque*.

Anatomy
The study of the human body.

Arabesque
A position in which one leg is raised and stretched at a right angle behind the other.

Telling the story with mime

Artistic director
The person who leads the ballet company and decides what ballets are going to be performed and who will dance in them.

Attitude
Similar to an *arabesque*, but with the raised leg bent to form a curve behind the body.

Ballerina
A female principal dancer.

Ballet
A form of Western performance dance that began in Europe in the 15th century. It takes its meaning from the Italian *ballo*, meaning "dance."

Ballon
A particular bouncy way of jumping.

Barre
Horizontal wooden rail attached to the walls of the dance studio that dancers use to support themselves while doing exercises.

Battement fondu
Fondu means "melted" and this step is a combination of a *plié* and a leg extension.

Battement tendu
A movement in which the leg is stretched along the floor into an extended position.

Batterie
Steps in *allegro* where the dancer's legs beat together in the air such as in a *brisé volé*.

Benesh Notation
System of recording dance steps, invented by Joan and Rudolf Benesh in 1955.

Brisé volé
One foot beats against the other in a step that resembles hovering in flight.

Cast list
List of dancers who will appear in a ballet and the roles they dance.

Character dance
Comes from traditional or folk dance. Included in some ballets, such as the Mazurka in *Coppélia* or the Maypole Dance in *La Fille mal gardée*.

Choreographer
Person who has the idea for the ballet and then arranges the steps and movements.

Choreography
The steps and movements that make up a ballet.

Classical
The purest form of ballet technique. Also the period in ballet at the end of the 19th century when many important ballets were created.

Coda
Final section and climax to a classical *pas de deux*.

Composer
A person who writes music, for example for a ballet.

Contemporary dance
A dance style that evolved in the 20th century. It has no *pointe* work, uses flexed feet, and places less emphasis on turnout.

Corps de ballet
Dancers who perform together as a group, but who do not dance solos.

Coryphée
In a ballet company, this is the rank between *corps de ballet* and soloist.

Croisé
The leg nearest the audience is placed in front of a position facing the corner.

Devant and derrière
Positions in ballet are either *devant*, in front of the body, or *derrière*, behind.

Développé
A position in which the leg is slowly unfolded into an extended position to the front, back, or side of the body.

Divertissement
Short dances in a ballet that do not tell the story, but are displays of virtuosity.

Ecarté
"Separated" or "thrown wide apart": the body is placed diagonally to the audience.

Echappée
Means "escaped." The legs move apart in a *relevé* or jump (*sauté*).

Effacée
Means "shaded," and describes a position where the body is turned away, with the leg farthest from the audience extended.

Elévation
The height a dancer can jump in *allegro*.

Enchaînement
A series of steps linked together in a repeatable sequence.

En croix
To the front, the side, the back, and to the side again, in the shape of a cross.

En dedans
Toward the supporting leg.

En dehors
Away from the supporting leg.

En face
A position facing the front, or the audience.

Epaulement
A graceful placing of the shoulders and neck at an angle to the audience. Used in *port de bras*.

Extension
The ability to raise and hold the leg high in the air in *arabesque* or *développé*.

Grand jeté
A jump from one leg to the other with legs outstretched.

Labanotation
System of recording or notating steps developed by Rudolf Laban in the 1920s.

Pas de deux

Line
Graceful curves and shapes made by the dancer's body.

Mime
A language that is composed of gesture and movement.

Musicality
The ability to dance rhythmically and interpret the music with sensitivity.

Notator
Person who writes down and records all the steps and movements of a ballet.

Pas de deux
A dance for two people.

Petit battement
The foot moves very quickly backward and forward close to the supporting leg. Used to prepare for beating steps.

Physiotherapist
A person who is trained to treat injuries and who might treat dancers.

Pirouette
Means "spinning top" and in ballet, is a turn on one leg.

Placing
Similar to "alignment," it is the way the limbs are held in relation to each other in ballet technique.

Plier
Means "to bend." *Pliés* are early exercises at the *barre* in which the knees are bent.

Pointe work
Dancing on the tips of the toes in specially strengthened shoes.

Port de bras
Means "carriage of the arms." Describes the movement of arms in a continuous flow through a series of positions.

Première
First performance of a ballet.

Principal
The highest rank that a dancer in a ballet company can reach.

Program
A printed booklet offered at a performance that tells the audience who is dancing and gives other information about the ballet.

Props
The objects the dancers carry in their hands and use on stage. Short for properties.

Prosthesis
A false body part, such a nose, used in stage makeup.

Repertoire
The ballets that are performed by a company. Students learn these works in repertoire classes.

Preparing for a *pirouette*

Répétiteur
The person who teaches the repertoire and leads rehearsals. Usually a former dancer.

Retiré
Lifting and bending the leg so that the toes point on the knee.

Révérence
Formal bow made to the teacher at the end of class and to the audience.

Role
The part played by a dancer in a ballet and created by the choreographer for the dancer.

Romantic ballet
A style of ballet performed and created in the first half of the 19th century that was often based on fairy tales.

Rosin
Yellow crystals of distilled turpentine (a tree resin) that are crushed to a white powder and used to stop ballet shoes from slipping on stage. Kept in a flat wooden box in the studio or beside the stage.

Scenery
Part of the stage set or design. Includes backdrops, which hang at the back of the stage, and wings, which stand at the side.

Score
The complete notation of steps or notes of music for a ballet.

Seconde, à la
To the side, or second position.

Soloist
One of the ranks in a ballet company. A dancer who dances alone.

Technique
The features that are important in Classical ballet, such as turnout and *pointe* work, and the dancer's ability to perform them.

Temps de poisson
A leap in the air in which the body curves so that it resembles a fish (*poisson*).

Turnout
The way the dancer's leg is turned out from the hip joint so that certain movements can be performed more easily.

Tutu
Skirt made of gathered net, either calf length or much shorter.

Understudy
Also called a "cover," this dancer learns a role so that she or he can dance it if another dancer is ill or has an injury.

Virtuoso
A performer or performance of brilliant technical skill.

Retiré en pointe

Index

Useful addresses

American Ballet Theatre
890 Broadway
New York,
NY 10003

Ballet Hispanico of New York
(Company and School)
167 West 89th Street
New York, NY 10024

Ballet West
50 West 200 South
Salt Lake City, UT 84101

Cincinnati Ballet/
School of Cincinnati Ballet
1555 Central Parkway
Cincinnati, OH 45214

Dance Notation Bureau
31 West 21st Street
New York, NY 10010

Dance Theatre of Harlem/School
of the Dance Theatre of Harlem
466 West 152nd Street
New York, NY 10031

Houston Ballet Company/
Houston Ballet Academy
1916 West Gray
Houston, TX 77019

Isadora Duncan Foundation for
Contemporary Dance
141 West 26th Street
New York, NY 10001

The Joffrey Ballet of Chicago
70 East Lake Street, Suite #1300
Chicago, IL 60601

Joffrey Ballet School
434 Avenue of the Americas
New York, NY 10011

New York City Ballet/
School of American Ballet
20 Lincoln Center
New York, NY 10023

North Carolina Dance Theatre/
DancePlace
800 North College Street
Charlotte, NC 28206

Pacific Northwest Ballet/
Pacific Northwest Ballet School
301 Mercer Street
Seattle, WA 98109

Pennsylvania Ballet/
Rock School of the Pennsylvania Ballet
1101 South Broad Street
Philadelphia, PA 19147

Pittsburgh Ballet Theatre/
Pittsburgh Ballet Theatre School
2900 Liberty Avenue
Pittsburgh, PA 15201-1500

San Francisco Ballet/
San Francisco Ballet School
455 Franklin Street
San Francisco, CA 94102

The Washington Ballet/
The Washington School of Ballet
3515 Wisconsin Avenue, NW
Washington, DC 20016

Acknowledgments

Dorling Kindersley would like to thank the following people for their help in the production of this book:

All the students and staff at English National Ballet School for their invaluable advice and cooperation, in particular Kathryn Wade, Laura Lavender, Antony Dowson, Dominique Franchetti, Moira McCormack, and Elizabeth Marshall, and the dancers: Joanna Moriel Muñoz, Désirée Ballantyne-Grove, Alexis Oliveira, Hiroto Saito, and Dario Mealli; Richard Shaw and Jim Fletcher at English National Ballet for their involvement in the project; Fox Charles H. Ltd for supplying the makeup on pp 32–33; English National Ballet's makeup artist Sarah Nash, for applying the makeup on pp 32–33; Dancia International (London), Freeds of London, and Wear-moi, suppliers of dance wear; Liz Cunliffe of The Benesh Institute and Jean Jarrell of The Laban Centre for their contribution to page 39.

Picture credits
The publisher would like to thank the following for their kind permission to reproduce their photographs:

a=above, c=center, b=below, l=left, r=right, t=top

Catherine Ashmore 26–7t, 53tl; Patrick Baldwin 25tc & cb, 26cr, 28cr, br, & bl, 30bl & bc, 33c & cr; Camera Press 38bl, Anthony Crickmay 43 (main pic); Jean-Loup Charmet 42tr; Andrew Cockrill 38cr, 55cr; Dee Conway 31, 53tr, 56cr; Corbis Bettmann 37tl; Bill Cooper/Royal Opera House 41tr; Bill Cooper 57cl; Costas 24br, 55l & tr; Dancing Times 49tl & r; Zoe Dominic 38bl, 40tr, 41tl, 42bl, & cl; Kobal Collection 40br; Colette Masson/Enguerand 24c, 39tc, 41bl, 43tr, 42–3b, 55br, 56bl; Mary Evans Picture Library 37tc, 48tl, bl & br, 50tr, br & cl, 54br & c; Getty Images 42br, 48cr; Image Select 48tr; Robbie Jack 30c, 39tr, 40clb, 42tr, 47br, 51, 52c, 56tr, 57tc, 56–7b; Lebrecht Collection 36tr, bl, cl, br, 37cr, 50bl, 54tr; Mander & Mitchenson Theatre Collection 30tr, 52tr; Angela Taylor 4, 20cl, 21tr & cr, 24–5c, 25cr & cl, 29, 30crb, 35, 42bl, 43tr & cl, 46cl & br, 47cl, 52–3b, 57cla; Board of the Trustees of the Victoria and Albert Museum 49bl, 50cr, 54cr; Visual Arts Library 54tl.